To Ruth -

Mind the Cracks

Pete.

BETWEEN THE CRACKS

Pete Weinstock

Tangent Books

Tangent Books

Between The Cracks
First published 2024 by Tangent Books

Tangent Books
31 Balmain Street, Bristol BS4 3DB
www.tangentbooks.co.uk
richard@tangentbooks.co.uk

ISBN 978-1-914345-35-7
Author: Pete Weinstock

Design: Joe Burt

Front cover: Turbo Island painting by Pete Ejuone, photo by Mike Stuart

Content notice: This collection explores themes of a sensitive nature including homelessness, problematic use of drugs and alcohol, death and bereavement, loss and grief, including drug and alcohol related death and suicide.

Copyright: Pete Weinstock/Tangent Books. All rights reserved

Pete Weinstock has asserted his right under the Copyright, Designs and Patents Act of 1988 to be identified as the author of this work. This book may not be reproduced or transmitted in any form or by any means without the prior written consent of the publisher, except by a reviewer who wishes to quote brief passages in connection with a review written in a newspaper or magazine or broadcast on television, radio or on the internet.

A CIP record of this book is available at the British Library.

Printed by CMP, Poole, on paper from a sustainable source.

Dedication

This collection is dedicated to Maggie Telfer (1959-2023) co-founder and CEO of Bristol Drugs Project (BDP), to celebrate her life's work and the ongoing determination of BDP in supporting thousands of lives represented in this collection.

Maggie believed in action; action without a fuss that had big effects; she made things happen, and she made things better. She created appropriate services to meet the needs of people who use drugs in a problematic way, and to reduce the harm to individuals, families, and the wider community. Maggie embodied 'radical compassion'. She didn't just feel empathy, she worked tirelessly to reduce health inequalities and promote human rights and so alleviate the pain and suffering of others.

Maggie spoke out, clearly and courageously, to challenge the malignant stigma and social injustice that keeps people who use drugs and alcohol in a problematic way marginalised.

She guided BDP to become successful and influential in the field of drug treatment and she sustained the organisation through some very hard times. She inspired and encouraged her staff to champion those who needed BDPs services. Her commitment was unwavering.

Perhaps Maggie can be characterised by the image of a solitary attic light burning late into the night, ensuring people whose lives are affected by drug and alcohol use are never forgotten.

Thanks to

Many people, for years of encouragement and contribution.

My Secret Poetry Publication Group (you know who you are); also to Martin, Jim and John in the MPG, to the Bristol Stanza Poets, and the Lansdown Poets, and to Richard, Helen, Martin, Rachel and Naomi for their work on the manuscript, and Jeanette and to the other Richard and of course Peter for his permission to use his painting for the cover.

I would also like to say thank you to the friends and colleagues, and all the people I have met along the way, for their support and friendship which has made life and work so enjoyable, and express my respect and appreciation to all the people who have shared their stories with me over the years.

And to Mary and Morris, and my brothers, and to Rob and Josh and most of all thanks to Kate for everything, and especially her patience.

Author's note

Between the cracks is a collection of writing that has a specific purpose; to shine a light on some of the experiences and lifestyles, and sometimes the deaths of people who occupy the harmful margins of our communities. Very rarely do people choose to inhabit these regions of society and I am reasonably sure that anyone who says otherwise has chosen to avoid looking at reality.

This collection is a reflective perspective about many lives, many stories, some I've heard, witnessed, or sat alongside; others I have lived through, many are true but they are not all exactly true, they have enough truth in them to let them stand.

I hope that anyone who might find themselves, or their experiences, in the pages of this volume will forgive me for putting them there. It is a compilation of glimpses, or impressions, of many lives and many stories, as well as some of my own. Any stories specific to an individual are there with the consent of the person concerned.

Pete Weinstock, 2024

Declaration

The views and opinions expressed in this book are the author's alone they do not reflect, or represent, the views of Bristol Drugs Project, or any other organisation or person.

The profits from the sale of this book are to be donated to Bristol Drugs Project to provide treatment and support for service users, or in the absence of BDP to some other provider of treatment and support of the author and publisher's choice.

CONTENTS

A poem for a friend	13
Strumble Head	14
Hemisphere	15
Rising Voices (The Recovery Choir)	16
Sometimes (The Recovery Orchestra)	17
Between the cracks Part I	18
Between the cracks Part II	20
An Island in the city (Turbo Island dig)	22
Archaeology of the street	24
Lonely as a clown	25
TV Room children's home 1977	26
Soldier on the street	28
That Spring	30
Perhaps time will sleep	31
Last days	32
All about the moon	33
Body Parts I	34
Oh, bad luck!	35
Body Parts II	36
The dark harvest	37
Starts	38
Truth	39
Body Parts III	40
Spring	41
Body Parts IV	42
Forgotten	43
Body Parts V	44
The dead of night	45
Body Parts VI	46
Body Parts VII	47
I want to tell you something	48
Time	49
Prophecy I	50
Prophecy II	51
The day of a friend's funeral in lockdown	52
Night notes in lockdown	53
Extract from the fourth horseman	54
The grey rider	58
The rainbow rider	59
In truth	60
Prophecy III	62

A sense of nations	63
Prophecy IV	64
Art a poem in fragments	65
Sir Edward's fall from grace	66
Prophecy V	68
Young Willows	69
Prophecy VI	70
A way of saying things	71
Firelight	72
Sowelo – 'rare find'	73
Three mornings	74
A crumpled heart	76
A Cheshire moon	77
The God of green wind	78
Chasing the dragon	79
The voice of the dragon	80
Voice from the shadows	81
The tears of the dragon	82
Wasted	83
Standing alone	84
Sharp Edge I	85
Sharp Edge II	86
Unwrapping it	87
Overcrowded	88
Not this time	89
The cold stab of the long night	90
He'd fight his shirt	91
The land of the Gwyther	92
Getting home	93
The colour of darkness	94
Mourning light	96
Echoes	97
The River and the Forest	98
The she-wolf	100
The business of the wind	101
Love is… all at sea	102
P.S. - for a friend	103
No-man's land	105
Just say: No!	106
Song for Maggie	108
My work my witness statement	110
About the author	112

A poem for a friend

Last night,

I dreamed a dream:

a train crash,

a soft, slow train crash.

I was walking alongside it

as the train crashed.

I think it was your train crash.

I just wanted you to know

how gentle it was.

Strumble Head

We each chose a rock,
yet they were the same rock.

We each had a thought,
yet they were the same thought.

Each rock was different;
each thought was different.

I sat on mine in a different way
than you sat on yours.

I thought mine in a different way
than you thought yours.

It was the same day
Yet, we each had a different day.

And we both went the same way
Yet mine was different from yours.

Your path, a different path,
though we take the same steps.

The view the same, but
we see things differently.

Hemisphere

Half the world
walking
I sit watching.

Half the world
talking
I can understand their eyes.

Half the world
searching.
When will I arrive?

Half the world
thinking
Glad to be alive.

Half the world
wondering
How will I survive?

Half the world
asking
Will I be believed?

Half the world
crying
Will I be received?

Half the world
hurting
Something has to give.

Half the world
watching
How the other half live.

Rising Voices

(Recovery Choir)

After Finlandia

Here are my hopes, my dreams, my holy shrine
A song of peace for their land and for mine

Voices from the city, wander in
 to hear other voices, and their own.
They sing for themselves,
 for each other, and the future.
Finding songs of strength,
 love, and sometimes sadness.

They come together to find each other,
 find themselves: discovery,
self-confidence, friendship, and memory.
 Surviving, thriving, doing recovery,
living beneath an open-hearted sky,
 in harmony; alive with songs and laughter.

Rising Voices of unknown heroes
 lifting to the heavens.
Chords of courage played out loud
 build quietly from a single note.
Each lonely sound swells to melodic love
 resounding from the walls and rafters.

Sometimes

(Recovery Orchestra)

Sometimes, if you put out your hand to the Universe, it will take it and keep you safe.

Sometimes, if you listen carefully, you can hear music in the air, walk towards the sound.

Sometimes, if you stand still long enough people will gather round to support you.

Sometimes someone will open a door and invite you in to a world of music that you didn't know was there.

Sometimes, when you're not too distracted you can pick up an instrument and practice.

Sometimes, with others, you will make the earth thrum and the beat of your heart will be the drum from which the music builds.

Sometimes, if you are lucky and stand in the right place for long enough, all the elements come together as the stars intended and an orchestra is born.

Sometimes, like a prayer whispered in the darkness of the night, notes and cadence will capture your heart and make it sing, and together you will bring the music of the Universe to life.

Between the cracks I

Standing over you
with an arm raised,
the face

poisoned with rage,
and there's the crack
of a heart breaking,

and your mother's love
can't help you
can't save you

and the streets
seem safer sometimes
than home.

They're a place to hide
down in the cracks
in the pavement.

There's a voice
the voice of anger
in your head

and another voice

crying out.

It sounds like yours,

and the heat

rising on your cheek

that burns like tears

like hurt, like a slap.

Only the crumbs remain

and the punishments to come.

Is this the beginning?

Of an appetite that's never satisfied,

a monster that's always hungry.

A monster that lives in a hole

deep and dark, a cavern,

of emptiness.

Between the cracks II

Streets ring with the sound of your feet
and the pounding of your heart,
then keys jangle, and the big door slams
a full stop at the beginning of a sentence.

Which is worse
The hand that pins you down
the fist that does the punching
or the uniform that laughs
in the face of your grief
your sorrow, and your hurt?

Or the punishments – past, present,
and future, or the anguish, the loss,
the sharpness of pain.

Or the fear, the fear
that lies beside you at night
waiting for the moment to strike
that hounds you in the daylight
following you in the street
shouting threats, and abuse.

Or the crack, that returns again,
with a promise it can never keep
safety and comfort, without sleep
keeping that fear at bay
turns night to day, the crack
that holds your life hostage.

Then the whack that cracks your skull
and the fits that rack your brain
causing cracks in your memory.

Then the crack returns
with the stealth of a thief
ransacks self-respect,
sets you apart from the world,
and breaks your heart again.

But there you are: a face in the mirror
still standing, still laughing sometimes
still hoping.

An island in the city

An archeological dig on Turbo Island, Stokes Croft: (2009)

They're putting in a trench, I wonder what they'll find.
An island existence, evidence of a long-forgotten tribe,
angry tears, plastic bags – thin as skin – that will last
for a thousand years.

They're putting in a trench, I wonder what they'll find.
Marked out in metres squared with pegs and tensioned string:
shoes, an abandoned sling, clothing of the streets
sloughed off in the moultings of another spring.

They're putting in a trench, I wonder what they'll find.
Forgotten memories, the jagged edges of twisted lives
unearthed. What else survives? Secret rituals,
ancient rites, exhausted days, tortured nights.

Paraphernalia: clay pipes, stems and bowls, shards
of drinking vessels, some perhaps centuries old,
bottles –Turbo, White ace, not Roman or Bristol blue
and ring-pulls and flattened cans of special brew.

Appointment cards to save your life
slipped from sausage fingers
and pawn shop dockets, dropped
from reckless, or unconscious, pockets.

Out-reached, out of reach,
banged up, let out, left out,
let down, out of step, out of time,
and, by social convention, out of line.

Roach-rolled scraps of forgotten lives,
lost spoons and broken knives,
lighters, syringes, glints of smoky silver foil.
They're teasing secrets from the soil:

An empty bowl of well-wished warmth,
thick as soup and twice as hearty.
Turbo island on Stokes Croft:
each day, another party.

They are putting in a trench. I wonder what they'll find?
Fragments, slivers of splintered lives – marked out, strung out,
smashed and broken, pegged out, sifted... and sieved
revealing how the Islanders lived.

Archaeology of the street

an inventory of things they didn't find ...

- Front door keys
- Buried treasure
- Deeds of ownership
- A secret entrance to Aladdin's cave
- The source of all wisdom
- Signs that Jesus ever passed this way
- The Well of Happiness
- Evidence of God... any god.

Ref: Post-Medieval Archaeology 48/1 (2014), 133–150 © Society for Post-Medieval Archaeology 2014 DOI: 10.1179/0079423614Z.00000000050 133

Turbo Island, Bristol: excavating a contemporary homeless place By GILLIAN CREA, ANDREW DAFNIS, JANE HALLAM, RACHAEL KIDDEY and JOHN SCHOFIELD

SUMMARY: This paper provides an assessment of the excavation of an apparently ordinary space in Bristol (UK) in 2009. Although the space appears unremarkable to most passers-by, it is unusual in being a place used routinely by many of the city's street-drinking and homeless community. Homeless people were 'colleagues', involved in excavation, finds processing and interpretation. The collaborative nature of this project goes further than merely attempting to represent social groups who have traditionally been excluded from heritage practice and interpretation – it lays methodological foundations for praxis.

Lonely as a clown,

I wandered, lonely as a clown,

through all the public places,

I'm not the only one that cries

I can see it in the faces.

They wear the smiles, those plastic grins

but the tears, they leave traces

Like livid scars, blood red lips,

a painted smile,

and perfect powdered skin,

these deceive the casual glance

but if you look beneath the surface

this veneer is wearing thin

Much is concealed, hidden by

the big shoes and baggy clothes,

and that bright, red, bulbous nose,

and a strange wig of orange straw.

It's all a disguise,

but you can still see the eyes.

Wandering about… this city of clowns

and high streets in circus towns,

looking through the windows

or listening at the door

wherever I go in this city of ours

the crowd's not laughing any more.

TV room children's home 1977

The light switch, brooding darkly,
itched to be switched on.
The audience of collapsing chairs,
 a battered refuge.

The carpet, wide-eyed,
 stained with tears and terror.
Curtains sealed against the sky,
 slashed, where light breaks in

through windows,
 smeared with smudged emotion.
A brick-wall view,
 and railings

waiting to be rattled
 with a stick.
The nearest tree,
 a bus ride away.

The light switch, itching still.
 A grubby pool of fingerprints,
choosing darkness
 to sink into.

The walls, papered over,
 pre-formed concrete origami,
hung together and folded
 to create the crumbling fabric of care.

The front door, down the hall,
 waiting for an uncertain knock.
three visitors: hope, doubt
 and disappointment.

A constellation of troubled stars.

Soldier on the street

You've done your time, put in the years; done your duty:
our dirty work.

No cap, no badge, no uniform now, to command respect.

Medals: lost, forgotten, hidden away in a drawer somewhere,
no longer deserved, or understood, you're not that person anymore.

Now, weak, ashamed, and wounded, you wear scars, not medals;
not all physical, but visible in the stoop of the back, the tremor, the
haunted eye, the hurt.

Muscle memory of the pack weight on your back, the gun in the
crook of your arm, and the miles in the desert sun.

Sounds and memories: last moments captured forever, distorted
faces and broken bodies of friends floating around you,

the twin whirlwind dust as a Chinook hesitates
before landing to retrieve the fallen:

ours: wounded, dead, and dying;
theirs: left in the dust or rounded up for interrogation.

Hell is not something you leave behind on the battleground,

You carry it with you – guilt, shame, horror, the knowledge of
what you've done, what we've done.

Your finger
on the trigger. Death
in your sights. You turn out the light.

*Kill or be killed, look sharp, don't hesitate,
don't wait for certainty,
react first, check later.*

The screaming sky: jets overhead delivering obliteration

and the whine and thump of death dancing in the dust around you, looking for a partner.

We buy a poppy once a year… you buy the poppy every day, or the grape, or the grain, or the benzo, finding comfort and forgetfulness,

even forgiveness, in the bottle, the needle, or the pill.

That spring
(Lockdown 2020)

When the world stopped moving,
only clouds sailed on.
The moon loomed ever larger,
making tracks across an empty sky.

Not much moved on the street – only curtains,
but the garden bustled, with a gather
of goldfinches on the sunflower seeds
and a thistled hedgehog snuffling in undergrowth.

Not much moved that Spring –
just shadows on the window
as birds crossed the sky,
and medication delivered to your door.

Things passed. Time did not.
It slowed to a mournful pace,
weighing heavily on the seconds
that barely ticked by.

Sleep, a shortcut
through the maze of hours.

Perhaps time will sleep

Days gently fade, mornings lost from sight,

echoes shadow the length of night.

The hourglass whispers, time slips slowly by,

second by second, moment by moment.

Time has patience for most things,

if we wait for the hands to spread.

Time follows slowly in our wake,

 or, sometimes, races on ahead.

Perhaps Time,

sleeping by your side, will rise up

as you lie in the morning light

and kiss the mist goodbye.

There are days, these days,

when gravity is not your friend.

Last days

Remember those escapades in sultry summer glades –

only the young would dare to waste those endless hours.

The perfect symmetry of innocence slowly fades,

for it is transient as the vibrant air of flowers.

Reflected moments, so fragile, so rare.

Purpose replacing fun, beauty marred by truth.

Gone, the gentle hues that drew the lingering stare,

and fallen, those sweet petals of fleeting youth.

Seconds laid out with infinite care by the ticking clock

All that's good is gone – even hope, lost at sea

or shattered on a rock, scattered fragments,

wreckage strewn across a distant shore,

the debris, flotsam, splinters of washed-up memory

as the howling winds of silence begin to roar, and now,

you're waiting by the door to hear that final knock.

All about the moon
(Wishing for my mother)

She carried the bottle with her always

filled with light from the moon

One day

when she could not breathe

and the pain was too much

she opened the bottle

and poured a drop

into each of her eyes

and one on her tongue

her eyes closed

shutting out the light

her breath came easy

her heart stopped

The panic was over.

(After Jaime Sabines – The Moon)

Body parts I

"Careless tongues cost lives,"
whispers the fading poster on the wall.

Cruel tongues cost lives.
They echo in defenseless ears
tiny brutal licks
dissolving self-esteem,
eroding confidence –
the tongue that stole hope

and the tongue that said,
'Let's nick that car' –
that one cost lives.

Body parts can be dangerous.

Careless ears cost lives.
Listening saves lives.
Not listening costs lives.

'I'm sorry I wasn't listening;
I didn't think you meant it.'

Oh, bad luck!

There are degrees of bad luck
an occasional mishap perhaps
'Oh, that was unlucky!' you say
'a beam of misfortune
from a full, blue moon
must have gone astray.'

Mishaps occur
of course, they always do
and accidents abound;
noticeable, not so much
when you're falling through the air
as, when you hit the ground.

When things go wrong all in a row,
incidents increase in frequence,
coming faster and faster,
events happen in sequence
and the very next disaster
looks likely to end in plaster.
Sometimes, you get this overwhelming sense
that you're in trouble

You know....
no matter what you do
you really, really know, that
the sphincter of fate is open wide and ....
is definitely pointing at you.

Body parts II

Other body parts can be dangerous too:

hands swinging in an uncontrolled manner,

holding sharp edges,

operating dangerous machinery,

or mixing electricity with water,

hands letting go of steering wheels –

they cost lives.

The dark harvest

We sow the seeds of fireflies.

They fizzle and fail.

We lose heart and die.

Bodies crumble to dust.

Dreams live on,

dazzling in the darkness.

The pen rolls

from the frozen hand, words

still warm on the page.

We follow the trail,

gather the clues.

Meaning will find a way.

Starts

Stops

With words in between

Absorbing shock

Channelling stress

A poem

A Crumple Zone

Truth

A double-edged sword
slicing the air

The spiny shell of the horse-chestnut:
Something beautiful lies within.

'Lies within'
that's a view of the truth
I cannot find fault with

A mine beneath our feet,
promising us riches

A mine beneath our feet,
waiting to explode, taking us all with it.

The blast strips us of our loves, our lives,
our happiness, we may not survive it.

The truth: that hollow desperate ring
when you bang the empty drum

Dry-eyed,
the children in the desert die.

Body parts III

Lungs cost lives:

lungs that fill with water

or with smoke.

Sometimes, time and time again,

they cost lives.

Teeth cost lives too:

biting off more than they can chew,

or chewing more than they need to.

Spring

Life, held hard in Winter's claw, breaks free.

Spring draws out buds, sharp as new teeth,

pulled from their gummy beds when Winter yawns.

Eyes, once sewn shut by icy threads, unzip, lids

crack to glimpse the sun, and frosted features

melt into a creaking smile. Spring held hard,

in Winter's claw breaks free at last.

Body parts IV

And eyes, they cost lives:

averted eyes, distracted eyes,

closed or sleepy eyes,

just-not-looking eyes,

those lying eyes,

'I didn't see it coming' eyes.

They all cost lives.

Forgotten

Cobwebs abandoned,
in an empty room
      by spiders hungry for life

Discarded
like clothing strewn
      on backs of chairs

Curtains twitching
from floor to ceiling
      wafting, concealing

Hanging, like drift nets
to catch the light,
      breaking in, revealing

through splintered
windows
      like new ideas

Quiet underfoot, soft dust
settled from lives
      lived long ago

In the air
a single mote turns slowly
      like a memory stirred

Body parts V

Legs are dangerous limbs.

They are risk-takers.

Wrong direction, wrong place,

wrong time.

Feet, too, are treacherous,

pressing pedals to floors,

slipping in high-risk situations,

taking you out onto thin ice,

or between parked cars.

Feet cost lives.

Heads cost lives:

Facing-the-wrong-way heads,

Not thinking heads, forgetful heads;

empty, ignorant 'I-didn't-know-any-better' heads,

all guilty as charged. They all cost lives.

The dead of night

In the dead of night

the slow moving quiet

of the hours,

all I can hear

is the hair growing on my head

and the sound of bed clothes

wearing thin.

It's a harsh quiet,

curving over the wing

of a swooping owl,

or the silent pad of a fox

on its nighttime prowl.

Air eddies in the morning light

around the ears and soft wings

of a pipistrel that jinks in flight.

Body parts VI

Ah! But it's the fingers that light the cigarette,

or carry the bottle to the willing lips,

or pick up the pill and place it in the unsuspecting mouth.

It is the fingers that hold the smoking gun beside the lifeless body.

Fingers have taken so many lives. They are guilty,

perhaps, more so than any other body part.

But not the thumb. The thumb is innocent.

It just happened to be at the scene of the crime.

Body parts VII

Hearts can be lethal too:

closed hearts,

careless hearts,

broken hearts,

hearts: losing faith,

losing time, or hope,

or losing the beat.

They all cost lives.

I want to tell you something

The day they dropped the poetry bomb,

a drone could be heard on the air,

it got closer and louder,

then exploded in our ears.

All meaning was compressed,

possibilities expanded,

shock-waves of rhythm and rhyme

resonated across the planet.

Nothing was left untouched

The Whole Wide World Was Alliterated.

Time

Where in the world does the time go?
Is it rolled in a ball like string,
or trapped in the rings of the trees as they grow?

Does it fly straight as the proverbial crow?
Does it collect in the puddles we splash in?
Where in the world does the time go?

Is it caught in the rocks below,
or stashed in a biscuit tin,
or trapped in the rings of trees as they grow?

We feel the ripples – the ebb and flow –
of space, its infinite twin,
but where in the world does the time go?

Perhaps it's washed downstream by the river's flow,
each drop with a bubble of time in,
or is it trapped in the rings of trees as they grow?

Is that why trees grow so slow?
A year locked in every ring.
Where in the world does the time go?
Is it trapped in the rings of trees as they grow?

Prophecy I

There shall come a time when the streets are silent, people will go not to the fields,

nor will they gather to celebrate the end of day within the walls. The city shall close its gates,

nor will they open with the rising sun, for no strangers are upon the road.

The bells will ring, but few appear, the doors of welcome are closed and the pews empty,

except for those few who fear not death. None will stop for news, none dare speak it,

or hear it, there is only death, death is on the road.

A time of great sadness will settle on the land, and the people will weep in silence.

N.B. What I have learned about Prophecies is this: if you are going to write prophecies it is wiser to write them about things that have already happened, you're more likely to get them right.

Prophecy II

Across the pond, nothing will be understood, all that is heard is the mouthing of words without meaning. Certainty will stand in the way of wisdom, and madness will stalk the halls.

The eyes of the world will not be open, the ears of the world will be deafened by cacophony. Stories, and the untruth of news, will drizzle from the skies, a place of foolishness and falsehood.

A throng, braying like asses, will mount the steps of the house on the hill, they will enter the halls like raging buffalo, to break the heart of the people, and bring down the law.

The thief, the liar, and the cheat, in the seat of power, will bare his teeth and howl long into the night, until he is consumed by his own venom.

The day of a friend's funeral in lockdown

The cat stretched out a leg,
then another,
moving quite slowly,

The rain
on the glass roof
beating, like small fists,

like tears
running down
the cheeks of the world.

I imagine the people
who know you,
moving quite slowly,

waking to the realization
that this is the day of the funeral
in Lockdown.

Not much to do today
but listen to the rain
on the glass roof.

The sky is grey
staying close to the ground
for comfort.

Night notes in lockdown

I

It's all zoom and gloom these days

reading, gardening, walking, talking

watching telly,

all zoom and gloom

My Internet connection is so unstable

I've been learning to talk Dalek

II

I hazard a guess at everything

teetering on the edge of freefall

falling, changing my mind,

then back again

and land gently

as on a feathered bed

Extract from **The Fourth Horseman**

We can see from the news on our screens that War, Death and Pestilence (disease and famine), three of The Four Horsemen of the Apocalypse are rampaging across the planet, but the world has not ended as was predicted in the Bible. Why is that?

My theory is: Victory, the fourth horseman, has lost the will to win. Victory, (also known as Conquest), is refusing to ride with War. In war, today, nobody wins, everyone's the loser.

We trailed in the wake of the hoof beats, and down the track we found
Swirled in a great black cloak, a rider, fallen to the ground
His posture spoke a thousand words: huddled in the night
His cloak, woven from the darkest cloth, near hid him from our sight.

We approached him, 'Sir, what is gone amiss,
Why are you here alone on such a night as this?'

His spirit seemed broken down, his body gaunt and thin
He had no strength left to fight, like his mind had given in
His face was lost in shadow, hidden beneath his cloak
His garb was strange, not the common weeds worn by local folk.

Beneath his hood a glimpse of silver, as he rose up from the heather
And across his back lay a mighty bow with a quiver of finest leather
He stood full tall and came with us, along the troubled road
He talked as he walked, and toiled as he trudged
He let his tale unfold.

Though I did not choose it, **Victory** *is my name*
Some will call me **Conquest**, *it is the reason for my shame*
A mighty horse I ride, white and pure and proud
Free as a soaring bird, or a drifting summer cloud.

With three other riders, I am charged with a terrible commission
We must ride far and wide to complete this appalling mission
We must range across the world spreading havoc as we ride
Bringing chaos to every nation, and devastation on every side
We are to ride to The End of the World, as long ago foretold
Recorded in ancient legend and religious books of old.

Conquest *paused, then he spoke again, his voice laden*
with a passion
Never, had I heard a living man speak in such a fashion

*'***War***' he said, 'vicious and cruel, rides forth with murderous zeal*
Death *and* **Pestilence**, *those craven dogs follow barking at his heel*
Though I wear a royal crown, I've lost the will to win
I will not strive for victory, not for saint, nor sin
I love this bright and turning world, destruction has no charm
I would gladly give all I have to protect this world from harm
The end of the world will not occur, though I must ride once more
The world will not end today, because **Victory** *will not ride with*
War.*'*

Then the ground trembled underfoot, and thunder seemed to roar
Through the dark and eerie gloom the riders came once more.
Reining in their foam-flecked mounts they stood before us
on the track
By their side a great white horse, an empty saddle on its back.

They were a vile and evil crew, when regarded from afar
Up close, it was as if they'd escaped from Hell
when the gates were left ajar.

One sat astride a pale horse, its nostrils wide and flaring
With a look of deep-grained terror, its eyes wild and staring
There it stood quivering on the track, little more than a sack
Of ragged skin hanging loose, with rolling bones rattling within.

The rider's skull had sunken eyes, his body was ghostly thin
More, a heap of gathered bones, bagged in see-through skin
He was a grizzled sight, the putrid corpse of one long-dead
I saw the fabled mark of Death engraved upon his head.

The next rider wore a mask of pain as if knocking at Death's door
A tortured soul, rank and rotting, fit for life no more
He clung to a horse, black as coal; its body riddled with disease
It wore a map of running sores with open wounds upon its knees.

This rider turned his sickly yellow eyes on me
He spoke in a rasping voice, *'You stare with horror and disdain*
Yet your fate will find you soon enough', he cackled through his pain
Watery blood ran seeping from his bruised and broken veins.

The third rider had no eyes for us, he was equal to any test
He sat a fine red horse, with the hilt of his sword in his hand
He was strong and dread and fearsome; he wore armour at his breast
His voice was the thunder of battle, **War** bringing death to the land

'What galling trick of fate has afforded this delay?
The End of the World must wait, we'll ride another day
Mount up. Mount up...   All sins must be atoned
The Day of Judgement is not yet cancelled, though the Apocalypse postponed.'

And away they rode, those horsemen; they galloped out of sight
Their hooves rumbled on, like thunder rolls, on a dark and stormy night
And left there, lying that mighty bow, the quiver of finest leather
And the glint of a silver royal crown, abandoned, in the heather.

The grey rider
(In a time of Covid)

Cloaked in shadow, he rides alone
We know when he is near
an appalling sense of dread
what he brings is nameless fear.

This rider bears no human name,
he comes with plague and war.
The fifth rider of the Apocalypse
he follows the other four.

A ghost: no reflection on the water,
nor shadow on the door.
hidden by a mask of darkness.
condemning both rich and poor.

Behind him flows a river of grief
hopeless despair, and strife,
thoughts of happiness fall away,
all joy leached from life.

In his wake, the reek of fear
heavy as a shroud,
a miasma of spreading fog
billows like a cloud.

He spreads terror through every town
with the wave of a bloodless hand.
The death toll mounting ever higher,
he poisons all the land.

Pestilence, Famine, War and Victory –
these horsemen are all well known,
but they are followed by a fifth:
The Grey Rider – who rides alone.

The rainbow rider

At first, we thought it raindrops
falling in a sheet,
or the sound of many footsteps
running in the street.

We saw our friends and neighbours
standing by their doors,
watching a rider in the distance –
they were giving her applause.

Encouraged, we pulled aside the curtain
opened wide our door.
Perhaps death is not so certain,
disaster not so sure.

As she rode by, her cloak,
which had been white,
broke out into rainbow colours,
a kaleidoscope of light.

She follows that other horseman
He, who brings fear and grief,
the Grey Rider – He rides alone,
that rider is a thief.

This is the Rainbow Rider,
her rainbow flag unfurled.
Althea, the healer, bringing joy
back to the world.

In truth

Truth is without emotion.

Truth is what you see
when you can't see anything,

but if you look
you can see a lot.

None of it, the truth.

It is all reflection,
assumption and
distorted perception.

What we want is:
(not the indifference of truth)

embellishments, interpretation, response,
recognition, forgiveness, compassion,
empathy, an overlay of human emotion,

a context in which we can exist, live our lives,
find joy, and love, sadness, and grief.

Someone has died

that's the truth.

You'll not see them again

the whole, hard truth;

but they will:

live on in your memory,

peer out at you

from odd corners of your imagination,

cross the street in front of you,

laugh in the next room

and ask you questions

when you are not expecting it.

None of it's the truth.

Someone has died.

Prophecy III

In the tenth house of a London street where wise and powerful men once sat, grown ups will play like children, laughing and dancing, while all around is silent and hurt.

Loud protestations of innocence will drown out the grief of the people. A fool walked in, and a fool walks out.

After the time of sadness, the guardians of wealth and power will scrap amongst themselves like dogs, snarling over the pickings and the takings; while the people bury their dead, and weep their tears, as they have always done.

Trust, and hope will be crushed beneath the feet of those who lead the world with false promises to guide the future. They are seen for the rottenness of their souls, how they corrupt the air and poison the water.

And the flow of coin from the clutching fingers of the poor will rattle, loudly, into the coffers of the rich. That is the law; and the poor will go hungry to bed.

A sense of nations

A sense of nations:
the variations
the obligations.

inter-relations.
The cut and thrust
beyond borders

in skirmishes and squabbles
over farmyards
and hovels.

No man's land,
where no man's hand
guides the plough,

or sows the seed,
except of his own
destruction.

Victory crows:
the defeated grovel
and kiss the hand.

History is written
in the blood
beneath the mud
of the broken land.

Prophecy IV

There shall come a time when the children will walk to a better life on a mountain path, crowded with those who have nothing; and beaches, where people bask at leisure in the sun and the sea, will be strewn with bodies washed up on the sand.

A marauding bear will maul its neighbour, but the nightingale, with great courage, will peck out the eyes of the bear, while the eagle and the lion look on. The eyes of the world will turn away as new sorrows spread their wings and fly.

The shadow of Death will visit the marketplace and there will be great slaughter among the dwellings of innocents. The mouths and stomachs of children will complain that they are empty, and the limbs will be blown from their bodies by the winds of war.

Fathers will look for their children among broken stones. Mothers and wives will weep in the ruins as they search the faces of the fallen for their sons, their daughters, and their husbands to bring them home.

All this, to slake the bloodthirst of shifting borders and the appetites of madmen.

Art – a poem in fragments (Tate Modern)

Life, a recipe torn from a magazine
Picture the scene: an empty bowl
Cherry Pickers have picked it clean.

Scallop-shelled, a cavity
where once the heart lay beating
A figure lost in the mirror.

Mille, mille foix: leaves in the forest
graves in the graveyards
all that grief, yet still so quiet.

Lost in the snow, sad faces look on
I dreamt the tears freezing
on the pale slopes of your face.

Jagged edges, so many lives
torn from their surroundings,
pasted, carelessly, into the pages of history.

The grinding teeth of industry
still grind: somebody, somewhere,
not us perhaps, but still to dust.

A blank white wall, three black holes
meaningful as any art: screwed, unscrewed,
it carries the legend: *Work temporarily removed.*

A desert sun, low and slanting
casts shadows across your sleeping face,
I stand blinking in the passage of time.

Sir Edward's fall from grace   In one Act

Scandalised Citizen: (*in a loud and angry voice*)

An outrageous act of vandalism against the history and heritage of Great Britain by a bunch of thugs. Historic monuments should be protected, they are sacred.

Narrator: (*in a disembodied voice*)

Did we celebrate *The Day of Shoes* when Saddam fell to earth? I don't remember a cry of protest about protecting historic monuments when he was pulled to the ground, clambered over and beaten with the footwear of the oppressed. We saw 'democracy', as we understand it, toppling a man who had knelt on the necks of the people until they could not breathe.

Scandalised Citizen: (*in a belligerant voice*)

That's quite different, and you know it.

Narrator: *(speaking with great passion)*

I don't often express an opinion, but today: this city, the sons, daughters, grandparents, and grandchildren of this city, engaged directly with the history of this city, they climbed with straps and ropes; they tumbled a long-standing wrongness into the dock. They proclaimed loud enough for the world to witness a statement of regret, rejection, condemnation. The belated toppling of an effigy worthy of a clifftop-burning, but in this city of the sea, they let water do its work. I say commemorate this action, this day when the voices of the people were heard across the world, this day of protest, a statement of intent, seen and shared by thousands. The police are to be congratulated, they stood by and watched, then rode away on bicycles. For once, they knew better than to stand in the way of history.

Ghost of Edward Colston: *(standing rigid as a statue, covered in thrown paint)*

My head is held high in shame; I always was too stiff of neck to bend a knee. I created opportunities in architecture, arts, and education, but my wealth and my name are stained with the blood of innocents. Should you acknowledge only my acts of beneficence, I think not. Perhaps one day, I can stand tall again; my name, while not redeemed, will find a new place in history, a new meaning, the honest heading of a new chapter in the story of *the taken generations*: stolen, enslaved, sold, and murdered.

Prophecy V

The winds of change will ventilate the royal house, and the countenance of the Queen will alter. The words of a new king will sound strange in the ears of those who will listen, while princes fight and argue.

The sun will burn bright in the sky, farmers toiling in the fields will see their harvests scorched and shriveled on the earth, the soil will turn again to dust, and the winds will howl, by night and day.

Streams poisoned, rivers barren; and wells – dug ever deeper – will be dry. Thirst will burn in the throats of the people, while in the gardens of rich men: the tinkle of fountains in crystal pools, and the sound of counted coin.

A change will come upon this earth: great fires will rage across the land, then come the rains, and the waters will rise up to drown the towns and villages, and cities will fall to ruin. The sky will be filled with sails, and the land with burnished mirrors.

Young willows

whipping the wind in the busy sky
saying: "Go faster, Go faster"
and the wind went faster,
galloping across harvest fields,

flinging stubbled straw high into the air,
to catch and carry, sweeping and dusting
like a house-proud farmer's wife
after the balers have done their work.

The willows bent and streaming
like palms surfing monsoon winds
on hurricane beach
as the rain comes in from the sea.

Cotton clouds mopping
and wiping the rain
from the wind-screened sky
leaving it fresh and bright.

Trees dance a wild dance
around the field's edge,
Outcrops proud and rocky
prance along the skyline.

We stumbled through gorse
from the car to peak:
tripping, slipping,
scrambled,

Our path
through rocks,
brambled and scattered,
across the sky-scraped hill.

Prophecy VI

The face of a wise man will appear to the multitude, he will stand among the animals, and tell their stories; he will carry us to the frozen world, to the dunes of desert sand, and take us beneath the ocean waves. He will be believed.

Engines in the street will cease to roar; the cracking of ice will be heard no more; cities will bubble from the seabed and cling to the slopes of mountains. The moon will be our doorstep, and we will journey to the stars.

There will be those who have courage to speak out against corruption, they will stand, or lay down their bodies, in the path of destruction. They will climb among the trees, walk by running water and the rolling sea, and speak truth.

They will talk of another path that can be followed. They will warn of disasters to come and point the way to a Promised Land where ruin is not so sure. Though some will lose their lives, or their liberty, ultimately, they will prevail.

There will be many who turn against them, who do not hear, or heed the warning, whose minds are closed to the future,
who will shut out truth because they fear it will hurt,
or make them poor.
All will be poorer, all will be hurt, if the path is not found.

There will come among the people new leaders who will guide them on the path into a future that is not broken.

A way of saying things

A way of saying things you don't know how to say,

finding the words you didn't know were there,

seeing things that are just over the horizon.

A way of exploring things beyond comprehension,

expressing feelings without understanding,

being, when you don't know what you are.

A way of looking in a mirror,

releasing your mind from duty,

lifting the burden from your heart.

Firelight

Thoughts
          stutter, glint and flutter
in the flames.

Warmth whispers,
          skipping silhouettes
trap blackness in corners.

Flickered light
          throws life to creatures
cowering against the wall.

Shadows
          wearing the skins
of living things

dance long into the night
          clawing at the edge of darkness
where fear begins.

Sewelo – 'rare find'

> The Sewelo diamond was found in Botswana in April 2019, the name of the gem means 'rare find' in Tswana – one of the languages spoken in Botswana. It is the second largest diamond ever found.

We go deep into the sky forests
searching for a hidden treasure.
Behind us, and below, we leave
the most precious of precious things.
We leave it splintered and fractured
with a ruined surface.

We saw profit, not precious.
We took the land. We took the sea.
We took the air. We took all the living creatures
and the spirit. We took them all.
We took the money
with the clumsy careless corruption
of industry and politics.

Neither power nor profit
have lasting value
when the Earth dies beneath your feet.
Now we look for a new 'rare find'
mined from the distant stars.

Three mornings

Cloud-smeared hills: a splash of spilt milk on the morning
sheep low and flat, too laden to rise to their knees
ruminate on the dull, green futility of their hill-bound lives
bracken bends and browns, broken on the earth.

Birds stay home; even gorse is pale this morning
the flowers, yellow and limp. Today the sky,
in low mood, has lost interest in the ground
pondering the meaning of light.

How still the hills on such a morning; the rain
hangs in the sky but doesn't fall; the trees lose
leaves slowly, one by one; they rest on the ground
and soften the sound of the next leaf falling.

Light seeps through: the sun picks up gold
from the hills; the colour of grass strengthens
lifting the intensity of the morning,
an autumn larch, a yellow all of its own.

The wind lifts: picking leaves from the trees

the first flutter of life on a dull, still morning

Then the putter, putter of a man and his dog on a quad

with a job to be done: lifting the gates.

The gather, yells of direction and pace

raising the flat shapes of sheep to their knees,

to their feet, urgent: a flurry, anxious to please

the field swept clean by the dog and his man.

Today, I see fence posts starting to grow

the wood takes life from imagined roots

energy flows through its twisted wires

the barbs, vicious as fishhooks, start to glow

new leaves, or Christmas lights

through curtains in a suburban street.

A crumpled heart

Crushed by things so terrible they cannot be said.

A crumpled heart, scrunched into a hard ball,

massaged, worked on, kneaded

into a more manageable consistency.

A lesson in pain, to lessen the pain.

Expression of fears, your tears.

Let them roll. Let them burn.

A Cheshire moon

A Cheshire moon

grinning: bright and wild

at an angle so jaunty

it makes you smile

Two black holes

barely visible

in a darkness

deep as forever

A scatter of stars

freckles on a clear dark skin

The sky is watching us tonight

and laughing.

The God of green wind

Cannubis, the God of Green Wind,
 sat on a hillside with mischief in his eyes,
he was looking out to sea.

'Soon,' he thought, 'Soon, I will stand up, and stamp
 my foot, to disturb all the butterflies on the island,
they will flap their wings.

This, will trigger calamities across the world:
 landslides, and tidal waves, cities will be destroyed,
and trees will topple deep in the forest.

No one will hear the trees fall, but they will disturb
 yet more butterflies; these too, will flap their wings,
and more disasters will follow.

Then, the world will know that I am awake.
 They will know the power of Cannubis.
They will bow down before me and worship.

Cannubis laughed long and hard,
 'Soon,' he said to himself 'soon',
but he did not get up.

Chasing the dragon

Prologue

It is said that in the land of Oblivion there is a bridge.
Beyond the bridge there is a castle. Within those walls
there is an armoury.

Seek, and you will find what you need
to defeat your demons: the sword of strength,
the spear of hope, and the shield of courage.

It is said that the castle is guarded by a dragon
and the tears taken from the eyes of the dragon
will bring love into the lives of all who drink them.

Our hero, lost in a forest, hooked and torn by savage thorns,
snagged and spiked on a tangled trail, struggles on,
alone in the darkness.

Terror spreading through the map of his veins.
The grasping tendrils of a choking scream threaten
to seize his heart.

Then he hears the voice of the dragon loud in his head.

The voice of the dragon

I know you are out there, frightened, and alone. I can save you from it all. My hoard of treasured grains will release you from your fears. Cross the bridge, come to the castle. Each grain is a gift that grants your wishes.

I will share my gift with you. It will free you from your pain. Come to the castle. I have all you need, a promise: of warmth, of safety and belonging, of all that you seek.

You can have it all.

I have a cloak to warm you and hide you from the world.
I will give you shelter on a hard road.
You will find forgetfulness in the land of Oblivion.

Remember, my tears will bring love into the lives of those who drink them. I will shed tears for you. I will swap your tears for mine, fair exchange. Come to the castle, find me.

You won't be hungry; I will give you everything. I will protect you. I will be there, always, even unto death!
That's my promise.

Nothing matters, not now, only what we have.
You are mine! All I ask in return is …
Everything you have.

Voice from the shadows

Long I wandered in the shadows of the half-hidden promise.
The mist was thick about me. I searched for the castle, for the
sword of strength, the spear of hope, and the shield of courage.

I entered the veiled world, stood in line, joined the army
of the lost, waiting at the bridge, to dispel darkness and fear,
hoping to cross the river of reality, into the land of Oblivion.

Beyond the bridge, I came to a castle. All was in ruins. I climbed
through the broken walls. I searched the guard rooms, the cellars,
the stair wells, the rotting dungeons and collapsed turrets.

There was only the dragon, crouched in the long shadows,
fashioned from equal parts: desire, cunning, spite, and fear.
It was whispering seductive promises, with tears in its eyes.

The tears of the dragon

In the last days of the forgotten year, glinting in the winter sun,
lay scattered silver scales that glittered the ground,
each one charred, scorched with the fiery breath of a dragon.

Now, at my journey's end, I stand in line at the chemist.
On the counter is a bottle with my name printed on it.
Collected in the bottle are the tears of the dragon:
thick, cloying, green, sickly sweet and bitter to the tongue.

They relieve the growing bubble of anxiety that threatens to engulf me. They ease the pain, assuage the ravening appetite, mollify the beast within. It has been a long, hard chase, following the erratic, blood-spotted tracks of the dragon.

All promises broken, except one: to be there at the death.

Wasted

In the wheelbarrow

lies the bloated body of a monkey.

It just gets bigger and bigger.

You and I, we're fading.

You used to carry the monkey

on your back

but now it's so heavy

you use a wheelbarrow.

Both of us are thin and wasted.

You park the wheelbarrow.

We've made space for them:

the monkey, the wheelbarrow,

and the elephant in the room.

Standing alone

Death stares me in the face.

No parent should bury their child.

I stare back.

You out there, you others

walk in my shoes for a day, an hour... or for a year

You'll know what I know, now.

You'll know,

there are no answers.

Tough, tough love.

Sharp edge I

(For A and others along the way)

Sometimes you choose,

or don't choose,

to drink, to use.

Your heart is battered,

bruised, torn and tattered.

Your pillow damp with tears.

Alone in the dark,

your mind turned over,

raked and furrowed,

a field of writhing fears.

You wake with a start,

a long way from home.

Sharp edge II

Yesterday

    the phone
    rang and rang
    in the empty room

Today

    high in the hills
    on an edge where the kestrel hangs
    rocks jutting beneath my feet

Yesterday

    ragged eyes
    behind listless lids
    dreams smashed to pieces

Today

    the rocks are waiting
    sharp as the needle in her arm
    for my foot to slip

Unwrapping it

Writing your heart out –
not ringing it out... every last drop
not ripping it out
unwrapping it, slowly.

Finding a place
inside yourself
to sit and think
about fuzzy, clouded things,
or things that sting, or stink.

Where truth and fiction
can spy on each other
without being seen,
peering round corners
at untold stories.

Feelings poured from a jug,
gushing, rushing
into a glass,
clinking like ice,
melting slowly.

A secret, like an ice cube,
hard, brittle, difficult to handle,
uncomfortable on the tongue,
a slippery thing, too cold to touch,
that won't keep its shape.

Hold it as long as you can
then spit it out.

Overcrowded
(A real event)

A convenient gravestone lying flat.

The body on the gravestone, recently occupied.
Not vacant, not quite, not yet;
blue lipped, still warm to the touch.

Moments away from a grieving family
unable to explain. Friends mystified.

A life, like any other, taking a turn for the worse.

The graveyard, a community
he had no intention of joining.

He didn't go there to die.

He went there to live,
to be held: safer, warmer
absent for a while.

Not this time

(A real event – continued)

A forgotten place, overlooked by faceless windows

Where some visit death, just a little, to find comfort in their lives

sometimes leading to the cold stab of eternity

Not this time.
Another life, snatched back from death

by Naloxone.

Blue Lights flashing in the graveyard

unearthly, then go out.

Life is killing us, killing us all,
some slower, some faster

some more than once.

The cold stab of the long night
(Cardboard city)

A ducked-down-duvet, a heroin-hide-away
warming, then freezing, the blood in your veins,
alcohol anti-freeze to get you going in the morning –

These saving graces, the twins of despair,
insulate you from the hostile stare
of a frightened city.

Loneliness, an ache in your heart, fear
gnaws at your soul, misery, a loyal shadow,
and pain, hot on your heels.

A few paces away, Death,
ever patient, ever watchful,
certain its time will come.

The long night pierces your flesh,
the reality of your bare-bones existence
is laid out on a slab of concrete.

A nagging need lays down by your side at night,
insistent, rattling, relentless. It shakes you,
wakes you in the morning light. You say:

Is that you mum...?

No, it's another day.

He'd fight his shirt

A man with a mission
to take on the world
to defeat it

He'd fight his own shirt
if he looked in a mirror,
and defeat it

He'd tangle with the sleeves
get a death grip on the collar,
he'd crush the body of it

in a vice-like embrace
and wring the living daylights
out of it until all is dark

He would wrestle it
to the ground
kick it when it's down

crush and smother it
break its spirit
destroy it

If he looked in a mirror.
He daren't look in a mirror
Who knows what he would see

who, he would have to fight
He's afraid of everything
in the mirror

the world, his own face, reality
the haunted look in his eyes,
his own shadow

Nothing to see there
only the past
hunting him down

After: Fiona Hamilton *The Fight* 'He'd drink his own shirt'

The land of the Gwyther

Silence rolls in to smother and confuse,
the path is lost. The low sky, a fleece
heavy on the mind in the land
where the Gwyther roams.

A veiled world, impenetrable, the gloom
so thick, so close, you can hear the blood
in your veins. So near, you can feel
the heart of it touching yours.

No destination. No direction. The way is lost.
The fierce wind bites at your soul.
Your gaze turns in on the black hole
at the heart of your universe.

Gathered clouds stretch from
the bare seepings of the dawn
to the slow dusk, that settles
like a washed-out shroud.

Getting home

The escape committee:

clandestine, bedside meetings

working out the details

lists, contacts, and equipment.

The right footwear,

an appropriate outfit

something you can travel in

discreet, respectable.

No date yet

waiting for the moon

to move through its phases.

Lying low

watching the nurses

going about other people's business.

Tunneling always tunneling.

Getting home.

The colour of darkness
(Trying to understand)

A future bereft of hope or happiness
Every hour the longest, the bleakest
A tunnel that goes on forever.
No brightness, no end, no distance,
or detail. Light, sucked out, leaving
only the colour of darkness.

I cannot carry this weight
it is crushing my heart slowly –
killing me.

It's not a choice I make, it's a certainty –
more an absence of choice, a must, a need.
The only choice is… How? When? And how soon?

Nor is it a swift choice, a sprint for the line.
It's been a marathon, a long haul, a lifetime.
The last few miles were agony.

Every painful step, the ragged breathing,
the pounding of the road in my heart.
It is a short step to freedom, a leap of faith.

The moonlight reflects on the water,
lighting a path for some to follow.
The burning embers of the setting sun

floating, warming the water. I dive in.
I turn away from the light, and swim,
my hope is in darkness.

Darkness absorbs the light
it smothers my fear. No echo.
No reflection. No me.

I swim towards the darkness. Oblivion,
take me in your arms and lose me.
Cover me. Conceal me. Hold me safe.

Banish the light – I cannot endure it.
Wrapped in the colour of darkness,
at last, I am lost.

Mourning light

Drowning in the silence of the never-ending night

Lost in that empty echo, the ache, the pain,

when I call your name in the morning light

the sorrow... every day and each tomorrow.

And yet, when darkness comes, it carries some relief

a moment of respite, of hope, however brief

that when I wake, this reality does not rule.

Perhaps an alternative tomorrow comes, one less cruel.

This other possibility might dispel the bitter truth.

So, I lie listening to the night with never-ending hope

of what another day might show, the answer to my prayer,

to hear the fall of footsteps on the stair.

With the coming of each new day truth creeps in,

seeps into my awareness to steal my heart away.

The house recalls the silence of the night

and the never-ending sadness of those empty days.

Echoes

Now I understand the holes
I don't skirt round them anymore;
I climb into every one.

The 'What's missing?' The 'Who's
missing?' The 'Who's missing who?'
Now I understand the holes:

the particulars, the details, the specifics,
the essential characteristics;
I climb into every one.

Searching for the shape of things
for the puzzle pieces, the puzzle itself.
Now I understand the holes, every one.

The resonance, the echoes. Suddenly
the words mean so much more,
and the silences – I climb into every one.

There are *enough holes to fill the Albert Hall*
I know that now… and what it means.
Now that I understand the holes,
I climb into every one.

(Ref. Beatles – Sgt Pepper's Lonely Hearts Club Band)

River and the Forest

    And there's you   talking
Here I am you say   *tumbling over myself*
And there you are   falling away
    losing yourself   in ever deeper pools
    New contours   and channels to explore
    You move so fast   you pass me by
    You ripple   you roar
    according to   your mood
    Hoping   for all the world
    to meet   with your rushing waters
    Shouting   *Come on,*
Come with me   I'll take you there
There you go   racing ahead
    eager to   journey beyond
    our shores   to meet
    your destiny   head on
As you pass   me by
you cloud   your light
    with an   alluvial load
tugging   worrying
snagging   at me as you go
I've heard   your stories
    travelling   ever further
ever deeper   Your edges
    lost   and forgotten
in the vastness   of the ocean
    where paths   exist
for the briefest   time
    then are gone   forever
    swamped   by waves
    that carry   across the world
    like voices   from a great distance
Your depths   where
    only dark   can thrive
your centre   deep and hidden
    no light   ever
penetrated   there.

```
                    I stand
                            waiting
                    pondering        the passage
            of history         watching   the years go by
         marking time   I dress      according      to the time of year
        inspired   by the light   and mood      of the sky
          I sing         in the breeze      dance to       the wind
       I wear weaves         of carefully      observed themes
           bringing softer       and softer shapes   with each cycle
       of the seasons      I pay   close attention   to every
          never to be repeated, detail        my life's work
       We have      no need   of harshness            here
             keeping         travellers       to guided      paths
       and strangers     greet      each other    with nods
             and smiles   Evidence      of their own    existence
       witnessed    in the eyes    of another.
                    Arms      outstretched      in welcome      openness
                         Come Walk
                         beneath my
                          branches
                         Be moved
                        by my beauty
                        and the birds
                         singing in
                          my heart
                         where love
                          can walk
                        hand in hand
                          with love
```

(After Forest and River – Zhaleh Esfahani)

The she-wolf

tracks through the landscape
the empty valleys
the lonely hills.

Hunger,
long and slow
burning amber in her eyes.

She stops...
listens... senses...
movement shapes the air.

The land knows she's there
ears tuned to the wind
eyes open to the skies

every breath or rustle
twitched through the grass
carried by the breeze.

All else is still
in hope
in hiding.

Everything listens
to her listening
senses her sensing

their muscles taut
as muscles can only be
when death is near.

Then, slowly rising in the hills
the shadow of a howl
passes over the land,

lifting, falling
filling the air
like the wings of a great bird.

She moves on
All can breathe again
She gives the gift of life
to every creature she passes.

The business of the wind

Sculpted, turtle-shelled trees,
dys-topiaried by the gnarled hand
of a hard wind that knows
its business here – knows its way,
by land, by sea, where it's going, and why.

Waves from other seas
crash against our shores.
In the breaking wake of the surf,
seals sink and skive
in the shelter of a tumbled beach.

Deep-cut caves, hooting
from the cavernous
maw of the sea-carved cliffs,
the floor littered with damp-jeweled
treasures left by pirates
and whale's teeth lost at sea.

We scrunch, scud and slip
on weed-strangled rock
scarred, kelped, acneyed
with small eruptions,
strewn, stranded,
and bladder-wracked.

Love is... all at sea
(With a big nod to Adrian Henri)

Love is   a boat: a tugboat pulling you in a direction you didn't know you wanted to go

Love is   a Once-In-A-Lifetime cruise ship and you, carrying all your dreams in a suitcase

Love is   the collision with an iceberg
and you didn't see it coming

>   Th
>   ere's
>   none so
>   blind as will
>   not see. There's
> none so blind as love
> It's the 90% below the sea
> not that glittery bit above

Love is   a one-way ticket to Paradise island
and you going with a friend

Love is   being cast adrift in an open boat on an empty ocean. You don't mind, you have everything you need on board

Love is   Flotsam finding Jetsam
washed up on a lonely shore

Love is   the first sight of the lighthouse from far out at sea
your love shining, shining out to me

Love is   finding the harbour of happiness
after crossing a dangerous sea

Love is   coming home
and you coming home to me

P. S.   (For a friend)

See how love

wraps itself around us,
folding in
to keep us close,

how it shapes itself
like a gloved hand
to hold us safe.

It is a shield
that protects us,
and those we love.

See how love

shines out like a star,
a light in the night
to show us the way.

Love is the path
we follow to bring us
safely home.

It is the fire in the hearth
that makes it home, and warms us
through the winter cold.

Perhaps,
if we let it
love will shape the world.

No man's land (The War on Drugs)

Wars
    are rarely won
           though many die

    In no-man's-land
        some wander in
            to find themselves

ignorant
    of where
        they are
  or   the danger   they are in

often
    in the sunshine
        of their youth
    hiding out   in no-man's-land

unaware
    of the shells
        about to explode
  above their heads
        beneath their feet
            in their hearts

How the ground will shake

their friends
    their brothers   their sisters

  lying
      on the cold earth

their voices
    silenced
        forever.
            They never
  went to war.
      This war
        makes casualties
            of us all.

Just say: No!

Once, they were post office managers, now they slink about the place, lurking on street corners with hoods up, doing dodgy deals, shady transactions, surreptitiously supplying envelopes, biros and the most innocent of birthday cards.

The authorities are coming down hard on the latest scourge to hit our towns and villages and our city streets: the buying and selling of stamps, sticky tape and stationery, and a range of postage options; now, new dealers are moving in on county lines, just a call away.

Respectable citizens watch on, regarding them, with sniffily disapproving looks as hardened stationery users come by to collect their regular supply, and young people grab some stamps and envelopes for a bit of harmless letter writing at the weekend.

But we're coming down hard, on these shopkeepers, these illicit purveyors of geometry sets and cheap toys. If we catch them selling jigsaws or photos for passports and licences, or setting up the unlawful delivery of parcels anywhere in the world (that's their proud boast),

we'll see them in court, intimidate them with incriminating evidence of wrongdoing, demand payments which they do not owe, condemn them, prosecute them. We've got them, bang to rights, we'll bring them low, bang them up, and send them down.

We'll ruin their reputations, their lives, their families' lives; remove that honest citizen status, turn them into outlaws because… they're criminals… they've broken the law. They're the new dealers on the block, bold as brass on the street, I've seen them:

brazenly delivering to our front doors in broad daylight, crocodile smiles on evil faces, with incriminating red sacks and jackets, identifying features, blatant as the dark tattoos of street gangs.

Song for Maggie

You witnessed the wrongness in the world but would not stand by. You never stopped fighting; where, and when needed, you lit fires. Standing against stigma, you challenged the world to be a better, safer place.

You came from the earth: starting quietly, building from the ground, a passionate adversary to injustice and inequality. Across time, you forged strong ideas and unshakable values; we heard your voice grow stronger.

With defiance and flair, you were always there. With character, tenacity, compassion and respect, from the roots of your hair to the tip of your toe, you held on to your principles you never let go.

Rare indeed, you were inspired, and inspired others, a visible presence, you led by example, always in the front row. You built services, attitudes, families: you were a gardener; you nurtured the soil in which we grow.

You blazed a trail; carved paths where there were none. You lived the music of the age, building a different tune, one that gathered the sound of the world around you.

You were the anchor, a rock to cling to, for those battered
by the storm. You stood out, the colours you wore;
sometimes, you danced alone, in the middle of the floor.

You were bold, and wanted us to be bold,
with the echo of your words ringing in our ears
'Be the best that you can…' you were always.

We will carry on the work you began,
in your spirit and in your memory
we will be courageous.

You didn't care what others thought
you loved the colour of life, the music of life,
you loved to dance; and sometimes you danced alone.

My work: my witness statement:

Making drugs a criminal issue, rather than a health issue has caused severe harm to individuals, families, and society. It is clear to me that many drug-related deaths are preventable, and a lot of drug-related harm is avoidable, the promotion of safer conditions would change the landscape of drug use. It would enable the provision of accurate information about drug content and quality, and allow regulatory control over dosage, it would facilitate shared knowledge and skills to understand and maintain clinical hygiene, and create better access to appropriate equipment and safer environments to use in. Careful regulation is, as they say, "not rocket science" it is normal practice with the use of many other dangerous drugs available in our society.

The criminal status of drug use and supply drives people away from crucial interventions and into the arms of criminality, the result is drugs are mainly used in unlawful, uncontrolled, and unprotected environments. There are many devastating consequences that result from forcing the use of drugs underground, these include: emotional misery, ill health and disability, social exclusion, homelessness, outlaw status, and criminality. The social and political response to the production, distribution, and use of 'unlawful' drugs has created highly profitable empires in the criminal world, enabling industries equivalent to large international corporations to be built. Every day, we see the harmful consequences of this on our streets, in our homes, in families, and in hospitals, police cells and prisons.

It is also clear to me, that The War On Drugs, as this policy has been called, is a failed policy. It leaves the production and distribution of drugs in the hands of criminal gangs and unscrupulous profiteers. This war was lost before it ever started; by creating uncontrolled markets and designating ordinary people, including children, as outlaws and enemies of society, we are sustaining a monster and have created a wild-west landscape for the monster to thrive in.

This unregulated, criminally controlled, profit-led marketplace enables abuse, exploitation, and violence on the scale of a global disaster; it harms individuals, families, and societies across the world. Making drug-use illegal has done little to control it but has caused widespread harm by putting drug-use, distribution, and supply beyond the control and protection of the law.

Resources on a vast scale are used to police and punish individuals and communities for their drug use and distribution. We are creating crime scenes out of ordinary activities, and gang worlds out of shopkeeping. Courts, police, and prison systems are overwhelmed by the consequences of drug-related crime. Hospitals and health systems are overburdened by the harmful physical and mental health impacts of unregulated drug-use and associated lifestyles.

If drugs were controlled and regulated, I believe that it would reduce the level of harm and the number of deaths; it would also reduce the pressure and costs to all those services. The argument that decriminalising drug use would herald an increase drug use is not supported in countries where it has been tried.

Of course, there will still be drug-related problems, but many existing enforcement resources could be repurposed to educate, inform, and prevent, or to treat and support those in need. The money could be used to provide the very important, missing diversionary activities, mental health and emotional support services for young people, and others, that might divert them to a safer future.

I believe that many of the lives lived, and lost, as represented in this poetry collection, would have been very different if drugs were controlled and regulated.

Refs: For more detailed information and informed discussion contact the Transform Drugs Policy Foundation in Bristol:
Transform – www.transformdrugs.org
Anyone's Child – www.anyoneschild.org

About the author

Pete Weinstock grew up in the privet belt, along that ill-defined border where the Greater London suburbs meet and mingle with the home counties. He says school, and he, mutually disappointed each other. More successful education came later with Social Work Training, an MSc in Mental Health and Addiction studies, and then a Diploma in Creative Writing for Therapeutic Purposes.

Pete has worked for nearly half a century with 'people in crisis' in a range of settings: children's homes, field social work, housing advice, cold weather shelters, homeless day centre and outreach services, community drug projects and a residential rehab, he also provided support for people bereaved by drugs and alcohol related harm. Many of the people he met on this journey were vulnerable, often living in adverse, and sometimes unbearable, circumstances.

Although Pete's experience is, by no means, all bleak, he has heard many dark stories and recognizes depressingly familiar themes. He has witnessed the struggle for survival and known many people who died; or who are mourning those who have been lost. Sometimes this has felt like standing at the edge of a cliff, looking down into other people's precipices or witnessing people being overwhelmed by avalanches. Writing has become a strategy for dealing with the intensity, and unresolvable nature of those feelings.

Pete has also learnt that writing can be fun. He trained in Creative Writing for Therapeutic Purposes to enable him to use creative writing safely in his work with others. Pete writes from random starting points, responding to his experiences, observations, and other people's events and stories; he has an unruly mind, it goes to unexpected places, and then dodges about when it gets there, often ending up in places that surprise him.

Pete is now at the point of retirement, he has brought this collection together as a personal reflection of his work, of life in general, of other people's stories, and of life in a time of Covid.

The money raised by the sale of this poetry collection will go to support the Creative Communities drug and alcohol treatment services provided by Bristol Drug Project, these include the Recovery Choir and the Recovery Orchestra.

Pete's one remaining ambition is to be a Poet in Residence at a cheese festival, he also has a feeling that perhaps we should all pay a bit more attention to Pope Benedict XVI's reminder that:

'Every economic decision has a moral consequence.'